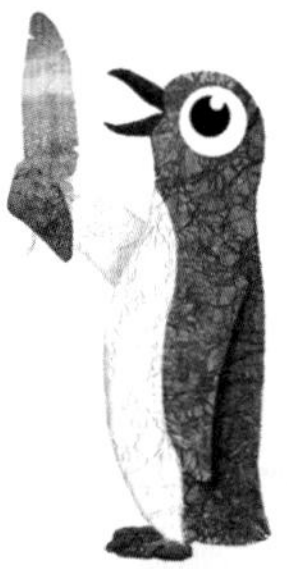

This book belongs to: *Addie*

Written by Alex Lluch
Illustrated by David Defenbaugh

Published by Wedding Solutions Publishing, Inc.

Text and illustrations copyright © 2006 by
Wedding Solutions Publishing, Inc.
San Diego, California 92119

ISBN-13: 978-1-887169-63-9
ISBN-10: 1-887169-63-6

Printed in China

Do I Look Good In Color?

At the beginning of time, Penguins were very happy.
They never got upset and they never got snappy.

But one day, a colorful bird flew high in the air.
And one of its feathers came down without care.

That colorful feather made the Penguins feel down.
It made them so sad. It gave them a frown.

The Penguins all wished they were as bright as that feather.
It made them forget the cold, bitter weather.

The bravest of Penguins then chose to find out
what a bird of such beauty could be all about.

He walked a great distance and swam many miles.
The colorful feather kept giving him smiles.

He found a Flamingo who stood on one leg.
He noticed the bird had laid a big egg.

He asked if the feather
was one of his own.

The big bird smiled
as he gave him a wink.
"That is a nice feather,
but my color is pink."

He then found a Jay bird who was all alone,
picking up sticks to bring back to his home.

He asked if the feather
was one of his own.

"I don't know what in heaven
could give you that clue.
That can't be my feather.
My color is blue."

He found a small
Hummingbird floating in air.
The tiny bird seemed to be
eating a pear.

He asked if the feather
was one of his own.

"That is the most colorful
feather I have ever seen.
But look at my feathers.
My color is green."

He spotted a Swallow
diving down from the sky,
heading straight towards
a blackberry pie.

He asked if the feather
was one of his own.

"That feather reminds me of
my cousin named Chirple.
But look a bit closer.
My color is purple."

He then saw a Canary,
so happy and sweet.
He was eating a treat
with both of his feet.

He asked if the feather
was one of his own.

"I like to eat seeds
all mixed up in jello.
Open your eyes.
My color is yellow."

He then found a Cardinal
eating some berries.
A quick and sleek mouse
was stealing his cherries.

He asked if the feather
was one of his own.

"I don't have a feather
like that on my head.
The reason for that is
my color is red."

He then found an Oriole building a nest.
He looked very tired and needed some rest.

He asked if the feather was one of his own.

"That feather reminds me
of birds down in Torrange.
I don't live in Torrange
'cause my color is orange."

He then saw an Owl
with eyes wide and round.
The bird with big eyes
was wearing a crown.

He asked if the feather
was one of his own.

"If you see my big eyes,
and my bright, shiny crown,
why can't you see that
my color is brown?"

He then saw the most colorful bird he had ever seen.
It was pink, blue, red, purple, yellow, and green!

He asked if the feather was one of his own.

"You're a sharp little Penguin,
so smart and so clever!
I am a colorful Parrot,
and that is my feather!"

The Penguin cried out,
"I don't think it's fair, I don't think it's right,
that you are so beautiful and I'm black and white!"

The Parrot then said, "There is no need to cry,
there is no need to plea.
I'll give you some feathers,
and you'll look just like me."

"Wow! I really look beautiful, I really look sleek.
When my friends see me in color, I think they will freak."

While waving goodbye the Penguin then said,
"So long and farewell, my beautiful friends!
I'll remember this day, from now 'til the end!"

When he returned home, his friends were so jealous.
The Penguin was the prettiest of all the ice fellas.

But then they discovered those feathers on his skin
didn't make him look good, didn't make him look thin.

The Penguin couldn't play, have fun, or a thrill.
Those feathers wouldn't let him swim, fish, or slide down the hill.

The colorful Penguin was sad and not glad.
This was the worst idea that he'd ever had!

He wanted to be white and he wanted to be black.
He ruffled his feathers 'til there were none on his back.

He learned a big lesson to which he then vowed:
to accept who he was and learn to be proud!

Then he went swimming with all of his friends.

And with this happy ending, the story now ends!

The End